JEFF GORDON

KENNY ABDO

Fly!
An Imprint of Abdo Zoom
abdobooks.com

abdobooks.com

Published by Abdo Zoom, a division of ABDO, P.O. Box 398166, Minneapolis, Minnesota
55439. Copyright © 2022 by Abdo Consulting Group, Inc. International copyrights
reserved in all countries. No part of this book may be reproduced in any
form without written permission from the publisher. Fly!™ is a trademark and logo
of Abdo Zoom.

Printed in the United States of America, North Mankato, Minnesota.
102021
012022

**THIS BOOK CONTAINS
RECYCLED MATERIALS**

Photo Credits: Alamy, AP Images, Getty Images, iStock, Shutterstock
Production Contributors: Kenny Abdo, Jennie Forsberg, Grace Hansen
Design Contributors: Candice Keimig, Neil Klinepier

Library of Congress Control Number: 2021940207

Publisher's Cataloging-in-Publication Data

Names: Abdo, Kenny, author.
Title: Jeff Gordon / by Kenny Abdo
Description: Minneapolis, Minnesota : Abdo Zoom, 2022 | Series: NASCAR biographies |
    Includes online resources and index.
Identifiers: ISBN 9781098226817 (lib. bdg.) | ISBN 9781644946848 (pbk.) | ISBN
    9781098227654 (ebook) | ISBN 9781098228071 (Read-to-Me ebook)
Subjects: LCSH: Gordon, Jeff, 1971---Juvenile literature. | Automobile racing drivers-
    Biography--Juvenile literature. | Stock car drivers--Biography--Juvenile literature. |
    NASCAR (Association)--Juvenile literature. | Stock car racing--Juvenile literature.
Classification: DDC 796.72092--dc23tt

TABLE OF CONTENTS

JEFF GORDON

With his aggressive driving style and knack for winning, Jeff Gordon laps all other racers.

Dominating the sport in the 1990s and early 2000s, Gordon holds records and wins that drive NASCAR fans wild!

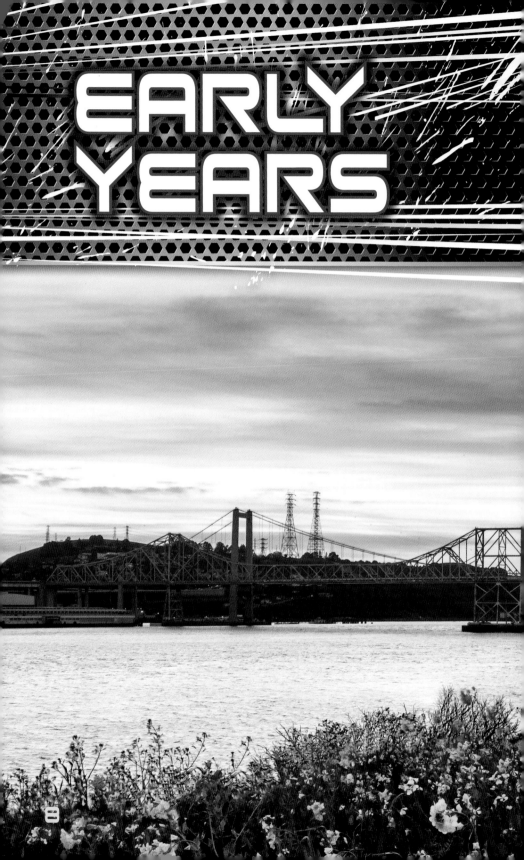

EARLY YEARS

Jeffery Gordon was born in Vallejo, California, in 1971.

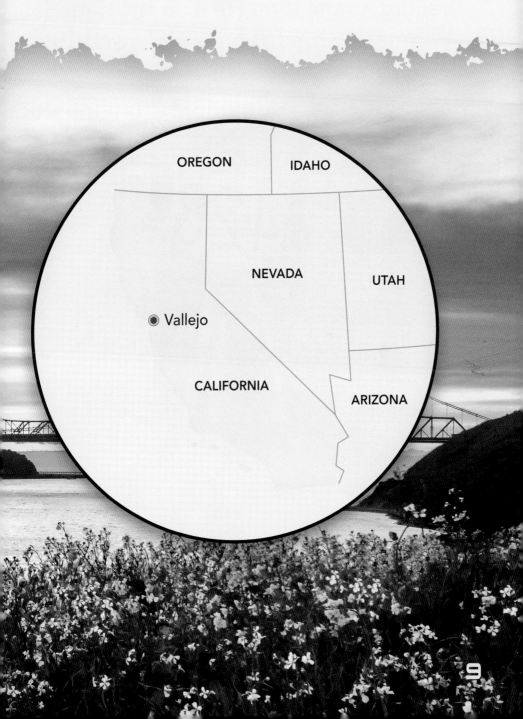

OREGON

IDAHO

NEVADA

UTAH

◉ Vallejo

CALIFORNIA

ARIZONA

At age four, Gordon was racing **BMX** bikes. He began competitive auto racing at age five. He won the national **championships** at ages eight and 10!

When Gordon was 13, his family moved to Pittsboro, Indiana. There, he drove in races that did not have minimum-age requirements.

THE BIG TIME

Gordon earned Rookie of the Year his first year of racing. The following year he won the first ever Brickyard 400! Gordon claimed his first season points **championship** in 1995.

Gordon became the youngest driver
to win the **Daytona 500** in 1997. He
also became the first racer to win the
Southern 500 three times in a row!

Gordon won his second **Daytona 500** in 1999! In 2004, Gordon won his fourth Brickyard 400 and the Daytona 500 again in 2005!

In 2013, Gordon set a NASCAR record by winning at least one **pole** position in a race for the 21st season in a row!

In 2015, Gordon announced that he was retiring from the sport. At the time of his retirement, his 93 career wins were third most in the sport's history!

LEGACY

Gordon holds many records. He has the most **Cup Series** wins on road courses with 9 and **restrictor plate** tracks with 12!

Gordon launched the Jeff Gordon Children's Foundation in 1999 to help fund children's cancer research. In 2006, he opened the Jeff Gordon Children's Hospital in Concord, North Carolina.

Gordon is the all-time winningest driver in the history of NASCAR's Brickyard 400, proving his tire marks on the sport will last the test of time.

GLOSSARY

BMX – short for bicycle motocross, which is a competitive biking race.

championship – a game held to find a first-place winner.

Cup Series – the top racing series of NASCAR where 16 drivers compete for the championship. The first nine races are three rounds, with four participants cut after each.

Daytona 500 – the most famous stock car race in the world and one of the races in the Spring Cup Series.

dominate – to have control over something.

pole – the fastest time in qualifying.

restrictor plate – a device installed at the intake of an engine to limit its power. Some tracks in NASCAR require its use.

series – a set of events in order.

ONLINE RESOURCES

Booklinks
NONFICTION NETWORK
FREE! ONLINE NONFICTION RESOURCES

To learn more about Jeff Gordon, please visit abdobooklinks.com or scan this QR code. These links are routinely monitored and updated to provide the most current information available.

INDEX